I LEFT THE BURN

Beth O'Brien

© This book is a work of fiction.
The publisher has no control over, and is not responsible for, any third party websites or their contents.

I Left the Room Burning © 2021 by Beth O'Brien.
Cover Design by Tracey Scott-Townsend
ISBN: 978-1-9163774-2-4

English language edition.
Published by Wild Pressed Books: 2021
Wild Pressed Books, UK Business Reg. No. 09550738
http://www.wildpressedbooks.com

All Rights Reserved.
No part of this publication may be reproduced or transmitted in any form by any means electronic, mechanical, photocopying, recording or otherwise, without the prior permission of the copyright owner.

Books have the same enemies as people: fire, humidity, animals, weather, and their own content.

Paul Valéry

Contents

I Prologue   **1**
   Certainty 3
   Candle light 4
   Sorting out 5
   Rooting out 6

II 'I always said I'd be a terrible parent.'   **7**
   Drawing lessons 9
   The diary 10
   Moon phase 11
   The garden's light 12
   Flower child 13
   The magician and her secrets 14
   Snapdragon 15
   Intrusion 16
   We met beneath an apple tree – of sorts 17
   Refillable 18
   Cutting the cake 19
   Her birthday 20
   Breakfast time 21

The Circus	22
Conjuring tricks	23
Trap door	24
The art of disappearing	25
Pickpocket	26
Back home	27
You'll change your mind	28
Barren	29
The penny	30
Deadened	31
Nocturne garden	32
Animal rights	33
The act of knife throwing 2.0	34
The birthday	35
Imagine remembering	36

III 'If old me could talk to now me she'd be wasting her time.'   **37**

Practise makes perfect	39
Easy mistakes	40
Don't.	41

IV 'I told you so.'   **43**

The ink from books	45
When plans back-fire	46
The balancing act	47
Rearranging	48
A match to a book is not a far cry from a bullet in a gun	49

Book burning 50
Smoke clouds 51
The packing list 52
If I had a ten pound note for every piece of shit
    I took, I wouldn't need to moan in this diary. 53
A tale of two homes 54
Daylight robbery 55
The escapologist 56
The act of disappearing 57
Smoke 58
Fast forward 59

V 'I write what never happened, I think.' 61

The act of knife throwing 63
A house of mirrors 64
Shards of fortune 65
The applause, the piano, the violin, the flute
    and the flames 66
I left the room burning 67
Toxicity 68
The smell of smoke 69
Send a raven 70
In the palm of her hand 71
Slight of hand 72
Siren 73
Surface level 74
You don't need to know the rest 75
I'm going to need a volunteer 76
Draught excluder 77

Paper wings	78
Taking proof	79
I name her	80
Hypnotic	81
Tightrope	82
Elderflower	83
Behind those eyes	84
Ventriloquism	85

VI 'This house is worse than a bloody circus.'   87

Letters never sent	89
Honesty	90
Burned letters	91
Unbraiding the sun	92
Your honour	93
Snippet	94
A beginning	95

VII Epilogue   97

The end of the tape	99
My first backflip	100

Part I

Prologue

Certainty

A bead of light pulsates as it moves,
travels diagonally downwards for the time it takes
a childhood memory to come to the fore.
The image is hazy, pixelated,
but that word doesn't belong to the memory
and the bead splits, creating two beads
that remain connected by the single word
visible in a slim line of light.

The two beads pulsate and move in different directions,
dividing upon division until there is a map of thought –
some of which is memory.

Candle light

She strikes the match and lets it flare
until she can no longer take the heat,
and the flame makes her fingers glow
with hurt.

Only then does she light the candle.

As she watches the wick catch hold
she imagines the flame biting at the pain,
digesting mistakes and too-honest words
until they turn,
first to light,
and then to smoke.

This way, they cannot burn.

Sorting out

She sees the loft as an elevated burial ground.
There is as much of her up there,
as they placed in the earth –
if not more.

Photos, clothes, books, notebooks, diaries.
Lots and lots of diaries.

She wonders why she wasn't more careful
with the words
she left strewn in her wake.

They bundled it all together and sent it up,
out of the way, like
pretending that climbing stairs reunited
her with the secrets
she must have forgotten to hide,
and she tries not to think:

Maybe they'd be closer to me
in the basement.

Rooting out

Deletions and crossings out fill page after page –
a palimpsest of memory –
edited by guilt and conjecture
until all certainty is blotted out
and I know this is her own version of vanishing.

I deciphered the tangled thought map
one word at a time,
knowing the truth would lie in the margins,
determined to root it out.

Part II

'I always said I'd be a terrible parent.'

Drawing lessons

I draw a map on tracing paper,
copying a map I drew before.
The first one was drawn in pen,
but this one, I draw in pencil
because I know myself too well
by this time to think I can do anything
~~without making mistakes.~~

The diary

I fill a whole diary with one day's worth of entries
because there are so many ways a day could have gone
and it seems a shame to only account for limits.

I asterisk events and detail alternatives
as a way of reminding myself
that our smallest actions
have consequences

until it becomes safer to live in a world of hypotheticals.

Moon phase

One spring I decide I'll only plant flowers
that bloom in the darkness.
I start with honeysuckle so the evenings
are thick with scent
that can cover almost anything,

and then I discover the moon flower
that senses only reflected sun
and basks in silver
despite everyone telling her gold is worthier.

She breathes in dappled darkness,
unfurls her stars
to create a basin in which she cradles
me and the moonlight
until morning.

The garden's light

I had coffee for dinner
because I wanted to be able to stay up
long enough to see
where the garden's light hides.

I let myself out the backdoor
and watched shadows outgrow
their living counterparts
until they'd swallowed the garden whole.
I saw the sun gather in her tendrils,
reeling them back in through the leaves
like the reverse of ribbon twirling
until the trees were only silhouettes
of their former selves.

Flower child

One rests in my palm as I hold it out towards her.
She brings my hand level with her wide eyes
and asks why it doesn't move.

Tentatively, she nudges it with her little finger
and it rolls over.
She thinks this is its belly
and I can't be bothered to tell her that a flower child
is more commonly known as a seed
and instead I agree that she can keep it as a pet.

The magician and her secrets

I read her a story about a magician
who told her secrets
to the waves
and before she knew it
her magic was the talk of the tide.

Shores became her stage
as she travelled the world in a sailing boat
calming rough seas with
enchanted songs that the clouds remembered
like a lullaby,

until the magician never woke up
and the boat ceased to float
and the sea passed on her secrets
so the magic could never die.

When I close the final page
she looks from me to the book
and asks where the sea
learned to write.

Snapdragon

I gave up on buying seeds,
instead planting half-grown shoots
because I'm better at finishing other people's work.

When she was little, they were perfect
because they always grew back.
But now we feel an affinity with the flower
that opens its mouth
when squeezed.

Intrusion

After two beers and a sip
of a strangers wine
I see the world like I'm watching
from the corner of my eyes.

I intrude upon moments like a clock that ticks too loudly

reminding everyone that time is passing

without contributing anything to help.

We met beneath an apple tree – of sorts

I think our eyes met but I'm not sure
and I turn away awkwardly,
preferring to be thought rude than mistaken.

I busy myself with the wooden pattern of the table top,
remembering that an apple tree under attack
releases chemicals to attract
caterpillar-eating birds,
which is a great fact, if you're not the caterpillar.

Refillable

I line up the empty-but-not-for-long jam jars
and relabel all the flavours.
> *Anger*
> *Guilt*
> *Fear*
> *Regret*
> *Winter*

to remind myself that what the labels say
has nothing to do with what's inside,
and then I begin to make jam.

Cutting the cake

I hold the knife with two hands,
my back to the wall from which I'd had to wrench it
the night when I ~~was glad I~~ missed.

There's a photo of him up there now
to cover the memory,
like a plaster for a stab wound;

I needn't have bothered.

Her birthday

The frosting on the cake was nothing
to the atmosphere as she raised the knife.
First in her left hand, then her right,
then with both as she held it out before her.

Soap bubbles dripped from the handle and he said:
you could at least use one I haven't just washed.

She said:
you could at least learn to dry up.

Breakfast time

I make him his breakfast for the quiet life.
It rains when he enters.
Sometimes there is even a thunderclap
so loud I drop the saucepan
and he stands over me with a closed umbrella
until I've cleaned it up.

The Circus

She asked me if I remembered the time she and I went
    to the circus
and I told her, yes, even though I'd never been to the
    circus.

I spun tales of elephants and fire, of trapeze artists and
    unicycles,
of candy floss she told me not to tell my mum about
as she handed me two pink clouds,
until I can almost see the red and yellow tent,
I remember what I was wearing
and where we sat and how cold it was outside
and how surprised we were that the tent was warm

until I lost track of who this "memory" was for.

Conjuring tricks

Closing fingers around forgotten objects
breathed life into them
and I could imagine everything to be important
if I held it solemnly.

The first thing I took was a key,
silver and dusty.
I slipped it carefully into my pocket,
wanting the dust to come with it,
not knowing if I wanted to be able to get back in
or to always have a way out.

Trap door

I liked to turn up unannounced
to see in those split seconds
whether or not
she was pleased to see me.

Where did you spring up from?

She'd say, like I was a flower
she couldn't remember planting.

The trap door.

I'd say, as if it were obvious.

Some days, I could tell
she wanted to reach for the weed killer,
and others, I could tell
I was the only reason she didn't.

The art of disappearing

She's too quiet,
and I'm not referring to her voice box.

Like watching a storm rage
through double-glazed windows,
you wouldn't know it was there
unless you looked,
and without the howling,
it's difficult to tell if the buffeted flowers
are flailing or dancing.

She appears like she hasn't just appeared,
like she's always been there,
and settles herself like she plans to never leave.

Pickpocket

She's a little magpie
the way objects disappear ~~around her~~.
Things she shouldn't have been able to reach
or known where to find go missing
and I know this is her own version of vanishing.

I leave her to it, pretend I've not noticed
the ornament, earring, picture
that no longer gather dust

until the knife drawer begins to look too empty.

Back home

I dance around the point
like a young bird trying to land on a bird feeder,
weary, but hungry to succeed.

I try to bring us closer to the point,
wanting to land just right
when I ask her,
when are you coming to take her home?

and rebuff further vagueness
with the reminder that I don't have my own children
for good reason(s).

You'll change your mind

People are so sure of other people's minds
and I imagine I'm cursed.
I stare at myself in the mirror like there must be a sign,
a mark, a secret written somewhere to explain
why I've always known,
why I never changed,
why I never really lied.

Barren

That's what she told me.
She told me she was barren
and that there was nothing to be done.

Barren.

Or –

Maybe it wasn't that word exactly, no.

But it's what she meant. I'm sure.

Exactly?

She said

we can't have children.

The penny

I take the penny off the shelf and approach the mirror.
With it, I transform each random scratch
into a petal,
or a leaf;
I draw a bird across my stomach with its wings
stretching to my hip bones,
and turn a spiral into a hurrying snail.

Every scratch causes a refraction of light
until it looks like I am sparkling.

Deadened

The room is full of butterflies
and her mum's voice speaks inside my head:
Anything growing in the wrong place is a weed.

I watch the butterflies I never asked for fly
trying to work out how to live my life
without having to let them die,

but I can't.

I also can't face seeing their bright colours deadened,
things that could have been beautiful let loose in the
      worst way,
until they are irretrievable – also in the worst way.

One by one, I set them free.

One by one, they disappear
until all that is left is the empty room
and I think about planting stinging nettles.

Nocturne garden

The wind chimes get tangled in the breeze
and the moonlight
until their delicate tinkle becomes an unearthly clank.

Somewhere, there is a fox screaming
and a lonely owl waits for a mate to call back
and a young woman watches
an old woman from a dark window;
when everyone thinks
everyone else is asleep
but they're all awake for the same reason.

Animal rights

I hold her hand as she totters along
but it's taking so long
I pick her up and decide
she can practice walking another time.
She doesn't seem to mind.

She points at the bright tent
and covers her ears like the colours are too loud.
I try to explain the intricacies of animal rights
and the entertainment sector
but this just makes her close her eyes tight
like little fists.

Do you want to see the circus?
A nod.
Okay, don't tell your mum.
A giggle.

And she cries for the entire show.

The act of knife throwing 2.0

She's got her back to the doorway
and she's standing stock still.
Like a dancer, she slowly raises her arms,
her fists clamped around an invisible something
before she spins to face me
and mimes hurling the something in my direction.

The focus in her eyes is not for this room,
she bows low,
applause ringing in her ears
in her head

and I open my mouth to say
I don't even know what but she gets there first and unashamedly pipes:

Look Aunty, I'm in the circus!

The birthday

Her little hands hold the knife
and my hands hold her hands
as I guide her towards the cake.
She giggles with the new-found excitement turning six
    can give,
and together, we slice through the chocolate goo
until there are enough slices for all.

I take the knife from her, and she parts from it solemnly,
watches it retreat into the safety of the kitchen
and disappear into the dishwasher
where it can be forgotten.

Where it is forgotten.

Imagine remembering

Pretend you're looking back on the life you have not yet
    led
or not yet finished leading
and imagine what you'll remember and imagine what
    you've forgotten.

You remember her asking to kiss you
and you remember kissing her in reply.
You remember laughing round the dinner table
and you can still smell your nan's house.

But in the echoes of imaginings
a note plays in the background,
like a scrawl that's hard to decipher
but once you work it out,
you can't un-see it's meaning:

Who am I kidding.
I'd never have listened.

Part III

'If old me could talk to now me she'd be

wasting her time.'

Practise makes perfect

I call to me from the snack cupboard and ask what I want.
World peace.
I ask me to be serious.
To be loved?
I hear the cupboard door close and shuffling steps.

You'll lose your appetite when you're old so you might as well enjoy it now.

I say that I might as well practise.

Easy mistakes

This morning, I tried to put the tea in the fridge
and the milk in the cupboard
and old me chuckled.

The good news is, you noticed. You won't always, you know.

I want to ask her what she means
but decide I don't want to know the moment I understand exactly.

Don't.

She stops me before I begin to speak.
What?
Don't go beating yourself up for this.
Why?
Because, later, you'll do much worse.

Part IV

'I told you so.'

The ink from books

When I was younger, I liked finding
where the gaps between words aligned
on a page;
where precise lettering and accidental word choice
in rows of text
created white space
white noise
in the midst of a story.

I'd trace the steps formed between lines of text,
like following raindrops racing each other
towards the back of a car window
when they're driving too fast for them to hear you yelling
brake

and I'd tunnel out of those pages in the blankness
when nothing else made sense.

When plans back-fire

I save these. All these years.
I save abandoned books from wildfires
and car-boot sales
for those later years of quiet.

But every page I turn
turns dimmer,
distorted,
until the words are as silent as the house
and I think: *it's never too late for that wildfire.*

The balancing act

I watched from the doorway as she took two books
and tilted them until they met,
balanced together by each other's weight, and held.
She took another two and did the same
until the beginnings of a card house took form.

Reaching for another, she opened it and began
 mouthing
silent words as she slowly turned the pages.
Half way through, she stopped.

The slim book found its partner in a hardback
and the structure became a pile in seconds.

Rearranging

I don't think he notices or cares
when I begin to shift every book we own
from the living room, to the bedroom.

I take them one at a time
and I walk as slowly as it takes
for me to turn every single page
of every single book
before laying it to rest
on a random pile
I take ages selecting.

A match to a book is not a far cry from a bullet in a gun

This entry wasn't dated.
She didn't see fit to, maybe because some things are always true
regardless of when they are written.
and I pinned this as the moment – whenever it was – that she realised
she was surrounded by all the ammunition she could need.

Book burning

I sit in the doorway for as long as I can take the heat.
The flames eat upwards, so different to humans
and I guess this is part of the appeal.
When the top book of the first pile is blazing,
I kick it towards the next, enjoying the rippling wave
that follows until the circle is complete.

Smoke clouds

I close another door behind me
and the inside of my head is pounding.
The smoke clouds my thoughts
my lungs
my heart
so much
for a moment I think the pounding is coming from
 behind me —
from the room I just locked.

The packing list

I walk around packing to the sound of a slow piano,
played one handed with so few notes I can't help
but think I've heard the tune before.

Though I've been packing for over an hour,
I'm yet to put anything in a bag, for I find
that it's easier to leave myself if I leave everything.

The piano gets louder and is joined by a violin,
then a flute,

then the applause of crackling flames.

If I had a ten pound note for every piece of shit I took, I wouldn't need to moan in this diary.

That must have been where the idea came from,
because the tally began in the wardrobe.
Four scratches gouged with varying ferocity,
maybe to reflect the crime,
and as more horizontals passed,
she decided she needed a pay rise.

I wonder if she backlogged her record with everything
she could remember
and how long she kept the tally going;
until she'd taken enough, or until she could take enough?

A tale of two homes

The queen is proud of how well her colony is growing,
but she knows the time is coming.

Her food portions are looking smaller than before
and she had been warned that would happen.

In a nearby chamber, though she's not meant to know,
a second queen is in training –
probably being fed the extras taken from her own
 serving.

She knows that the price of her success is separation,
so she gets her affairs in order,
prepares for the flight to the new home
she hopes she will find
where she must begin again.

Daylight robbery

For all I hate him,
today, I love him for distrusting the banks
because I don't much fancy a heist.

Instead, I creep upstairs (even though he is out)
and dig around, unearthing dust clouds
that dance like confetti in the afternoon sun
and I take it as a sign, hear the birds trumpet
their unswerving support
as I open a box full of fifties.

The escapologist

I cup every key I have ever owned in my two hands,
marvelling at the fine line between security and
    entrapment.
I think about the concept of the safety catch
knowing no one is ever safer caught than free.

I lock each door behind me – except the back door
because we lost that key years ago –
and I pledge to lose every key I have ever owned
until every door is open.

The act of disappearing

I lock the door behind me,
expecting the click to be weighted with a finality
it had never had to feel before,
but it sounds the same as always.

I place my keys in my pocket alongside the spare set
and they jangle light-heartedly at my stride.
I stuff my hand in to grasp them silent
until their metal begins to bite back.

Smoke

There isn't a smell on the air
as I turn to close the door.
I think about double locking it
but I'm trying to have more faith
in the universe, so I don't.

My bag is a bit heavier than normal
and I wear it on my shoulders
believing what I carry behind me
hardly counts
as I slowly walk away,
imagining the smell of smoke.

Fast forward

My walk turns into a run
and I know that if I was watching myself
on a crime show,
I'd call me an idiot
because only the guilty run.

I slow down because I'm too old for this

A voice tells me to run
but I'm done being bossed around,
so I settle my pace at an idle stroll
and keep an ear out for a siren.

Part V

'I write what never happened, I think.'

The act of knife throwing

She is so little, she drags a dining room chair over to the wall
in order to retrieve the knife.
A hurricane tears through me as I watch her hop delicately down,
carver in hand and totter back.
Turning, she faces the scarred wall, and me, now I'm in the doorway
and I open my mouth to say
I don't even know what but she gets there first and unashamedly pipes:

Look Aunty, I'm in the circus!

She hurls the knife once more,
but this time, she doesn't hit the wall.

A house of mirrors

I look straight ahead and see the wall behind me
unsettling in its closeness
so I turn
see three of me
surrounding me
each face
different
from her neighbour

one laughing
one screaming
the third screaming even louder

I smash the laughing one
which shuts them all up.

Shards of fortune

I watch myself through the sight line of a gun,

the intersection resting first on my stomach,
then my heart,
then my throat,
as I walk towards me.

One of us is shaking.

The shards of the broken mirror
flash from the floor,
making my bad fortune beautiful,
and deadly.

The applause, the piano, the violin, the flute and the flames

A crescendo cannot drown out the blood
but it does a hell of a job at trying.

I watch the unfurling pool,
and the applause is getting tired.
This only sharpens the piano's staccato,
elongates the violin's wail,
pierces the shriek of the flute,
and hypnotises the crackling flames
'til I can't tell red from red.

I left the room burning

I left ~~the room~~, burning
with rage in my veins.

I left ~~the room burning,~~
with rage in my veins.

I left the room~~, burning~~
~~with rage in my veins.~~

I left ~~the room, burning~~
~~with rage in my veins.~~

Toxicity

I open my eyes to see her locking the front door
but I keep my hands over my ears

because I'm scared the pounding isn't inside my head.

Toxicity edges closer towards us
and I breathe it in like penance,
exhale innocence
until my chest is tight from holding in
the screams

meanwhile she sits calmly beside me,
looking faintly bored,
breathing more naturally than ever.

The smell of smoke

I thought I could smell smoke
as I walked round the back of the house
and let myself in.

Someone could have been having a barbecue.

I left the back door open,
walked to the front door
and turned the lock.

She was sitting on the stairs with her hands over her ears
like everything was too loud.

As I sat beside her,
furls of grey crept towards us
as I considered whether fire would be hotter
if it didn't waste its time roaring.

I opened my mouth to voice this theory
but closed it again.

She still had her ears covered and I wasn't as wasteful as fire.

Send a raven

The raven plays dead
beside the carcass,
trusting to its reputation(s)
of evil
to grant it some peace and quiet.

From murderer's soul
to bringer of bad weather,
she collects bad omens
like memories,
holds onto them
and uses them
to survive
by being
still and silent
until she's left alone
to feast.

In the palm of her hand

I snatch the matches from her gloved hands
and leave fingerprints like breadcrumbs
everywhere she went.

My heart races and the piano quickens
and I prepare to persuade her
that this is for the best
while smoke fills the silence
and for a moment,
I know this is what she's been counting on.

Slight of hand

She grabs my arm as I turn to leave,
her hand slides down
until her fingers lock with mine.
She gives me a squeeze,

but when she lets go
I find

I miss you

written across the palm
of the other hand.

Siren

She sits just beyond my field of vision
calling forth every negative thing she can
and it's not her fault most of them are men.

She laughs
and this only makes the men flock faster.

Surface level

I take a penny and scratch at the surface of the mirror,
creating hundreds of tiny imperfections,
distorting the reflection that I'm pretending isn't mine
because I don't feel like the master
and I'd rather blame the tools.

You don't need to know the rest

It was the middle of the day when suddenly
It's not
I'm a year ago
and it's dark
on the floor
and he's heavy on top of me
when he teases me for no longer being "chatty".

I'm going to need a volunteer

For my next trick,
I'm going to take you to the bottom of the cragged ocean
where the siren lives
between sea-salt weeds and fish bones.
Rumour has it she secretly thinks that breathing is overrated.

They say she's a wasted beauty
but all a man needs is eye contact
to feel entitled
and she says she's all about efficiency.

The melody comes up from her lungs
but there's a scream in the reverberations
which sounds like it comes from her heart.

Draught excluder

I take such a deep breath that I feel it
crack down my spine,
like my body's whispered reminder
that what keeps me going,
might just, one day, break me in two.

On the days where my limbs
are made of already-stepped-on autumn leaves,
she hears the dry rustle
and goes round the house, stifling every draught
with a brightly coloured towel
until I can be still, in undisturbed silence.

Then she asks my voice to fill it.

Paper wings

The crowd claps in a slow synchronicity
as she prepares for her first flight
on paper wings.

Her spine morphs into two
like the binding of a book
and sheets of paper crackle with anticipation
as she stretches them up and out
towards the wheeling ravens

and it was just like her to challenge them to a race
before she knew she could fly.

Taking proof

Proof is taken from the margins,
beneath the tip-ex applied too thickly
it crinkles the page,
adding another layer of distortion.

The contortionist watches from the footer,
gazing up at the trapeze crossed wires
of scribbled out sentences,
crossed out edits,
and she morphs herself into a question mark
before she, too, is taken.

I name her

Truth.
She nestles inside me next to Love.
They hush each other,
kindly,
like it's for the others' own good.

The space is tight
and I realise I will have to let one of them out
before my ribs shatter
and I don't get a say in which of them
is the lesser of two evils.

Hypnotic

She says I look tense
so she lights me a candle
and tells me to stare at it.

I focus on the flame,
wondering when fire started being blue
and watch it flicker
in a breeze I cannot feel.

It's so flimsy, so easily swayed
I pity it
and relate to it
and want to snuff it out
just to let it rest.

Tightrope

The tightrope runs in upward steps
so I know the further I go
the further I have to fall.

It began with a white lie,
which, colour by colour,
became a rainbow of deception
and strobe lighting,

a migraine of memories
and falsehoods,
suspended in midair
and disbelief
like a freeze frame
or (un)lucky dip.

Elderflower

Her smile exists in the wrinkle of the bark
and she breathes out white flowers,
black berries,
and lightning repellent.

She welcomes the storm,
beckons those foolish enough to be out
to come towards her
beneath her
and as they lean in
she listens to the stories they tell about her
and feeds them poison berries
hoping to expel their lies.

Behind those eyes

Fireworks can whisper if you're far enough away
and her eyes always held a distant fury.

She felt in a monotone
despite what she said
what she wrote
she was just as good at writing lies,
like journalists

sometimes she wrote what she wanted to be true.

Ventriloquism

I grasp at this concept
imitation,
hurl sound across caverns
until I don't have to open my mouth
to hurt people.

I bite my lip until it bleeds
and shake my head when they ask
if I use a recording device.

They love a secret
the longer it's kept –
the more blood it draws –
and I hate to disappoint.

Part VI

'This house is worse than a bloody circus.'

Letters never sent

I write you letters, like these ones here.

I focus on my handwriting
so I don't over-think the words
I'm never going to show you.

I burn a stamp, an envelope, and imagine
flames dancing from inside a postbox,
pretending I can smell the ink melting.
Sometimes, I think that's the only way forward
and I wonder if red becomes redder if you burn it?

Every letter I write is a reminder of why
they are letters never sent.
Every letter I never send is a reminder of why
I write you words, like these ones here.

Honesty

I always thought that honesty and certainty
were one and the same.

I wrote the words down
side by side
across a double page spread

out like a thought map
that would soon be obsolete
when minds race like raindrops
and pages burn like leaves
and smoke chokes like lies
and honesty means nothing
when certainty is a blur.

Burned letters

I knew she'd burn them if I wrote them
and I knew she wouldn't trust me
when I said her secrets were safe.

She would comb through my diaries,
teasing out clues
like they were contagious
and maybe she was right to worry.

Unbraiding the sun

Sunbeams filtered through the slats in the blinds
that gathered dust because I couldn't remember the last
    time
I opened them.

I plaited the rays one strand at a time,
turned them into daisy chains
to wear round my wrist
in my hair
to mask the smell of burning that clung
like indelible ink
to my memories
to her memories.
I corrected us both
until our stories matched,
flared together
in corroboration

then let the sunbeams fly.

Your honour

I watched her leave him,
grinned as she tried to run
(for about three hobbles)
and then gave up.

She held herself taller
as she walked,
bag slung over her back
like it was nothing

and I was proud of her,

until I smelled burning,
until I saw the blood.

Snippet

I took the scissors and made a mosaic
out of the evidence against me,
finding that editing wasn't as hard
as everyone says it is.

I cut and pasted over honesty
and confused her certainty,
playing tricks with her memories
like reading a fortune backwards,

and I recited what she'd done
over and over
until I'm sure she began to believe me.

A beginning

It could have begun with the flowers
or the raven
or the murder
or the birthday
and that's something they all have in common.

I placed the diaries in chronological order
as best I could,
impressed and annoyed by how much damage
they could do in the wrong hands.

For an old woman that burned bridges
before they were built
she'd hung onto those words
like they were the keystone.

Part VII

Epilogue

The end of the tape

My nerves lay stretched along the garden path
like the stepping stones they feel.
I follow them along their zig-zagged journey,
winding them around my hand and elbow
until I reach the end
which used to be the beginning,
take out the reel from inside me,
and decide it's not worth fixing.

My first backflip

I still don't know the difference between falling
and dying.

There was time for sound to rush in my ears
like a last ditch attempt to hear a lifetime of noise
and as the world spun,
or twisted away,
splintered into mirror fragments,
like the fraying of an over-wrought rope.

Strands of life played in static whirls
until they were no longer inside me,
and instead,
I watch others read my diaries,
discuss my memories in the court room,
take my unseen place on the jury
and whisper:
guilty
in every ear, just in case.

Acknowledgements

Love and deepest respect to Tracey and Phil and everyone at Wild Pressed Books.

Big love to all the poets of the planet.

SORTING OUT - First published in *Eunoia Review*, 15th October 2018

SNAP DRAGON - First published in *Mineral Lit Mag*, 1st September 2020

LETTERS NEVER SENT - First published in *Dear Reader Poetry*, 9th January 2019

About the author

Beth O'Brien is currently studying an MA in Creative Writing at the University of Birmingham. Her debut poetry pamphlet, *Light Perception*, was published by Wild Pressed Books in 2019, and her poetry was featured in the Black Pear Press anthology, *Pressed Flowers*. She is the Editor of Mad Hatter Reviews, a site that reviews books, e-books, theatre, music, and even the odd podcast.

She has had her poetry (and the odd short story) published in Foxglove Journal, Nine Muses Poetry, Dear Reader Poetry, BellaOnline Literary Review, Eunoia, Pulp Poets Press, Peculiars Press, Picaroon Press, and Bonnie's Crew.

You can follow Beth's writerly activities on Instagram and Twitter (@bethoblogs) and on Facebook (@bethobrienwriter).

Lightning Source UK Ltd.
Milton Keynes UK
UKHW011301180121
377248UK00002B/164